The Bicycle Illustration

Copyright © 2024 by Justin G. Gravitt

All rights reserved. No part of this book may be reproduced in any manner whatsoever without written permission except in the case of brief quotations embodied in critical articles and reviews.

To request permissions contact the author at: www.justingravitt.com

First Printing: 2024

One Disciple to Another Press, Dayton, Ohio

To my Dad, who taught me how to ride a bike and who loves cycling more than anyone I know.

The Bicycle Illustration

> DISCIPLE MAKING IS JUST LIKE RIDING A BIKE

Justin G. Gravitt

One Disciple to Another Press

DISCIPLE MAKING IS JUST LIKE RIDING A BIKE

Pastors and Christian leaders all over the world are asking the same question, "How do we get everyday people to make disciples?"

A recent Barna study commissioned by The Navigators shed light on what keeps Christians from making disciples. When Barna asked Christians who weren't making disciples why they weren't, the top three reasons were:

22% "I just haven't thought about it."

24% "No one has suggested it / asked me."

37% "Don't think I'm am qualified / equipped."[1]

We can view these three as a staircase. First, Christians don't make disciples because they haven't thought about it. Next, there are others who have perhaps considered it, but no one has asked them to or suggested they do it. Finally, the largest percentage is made up of people who have at least thought about it, and perhaps been asked, but they just don't think they are qualified or equipped.

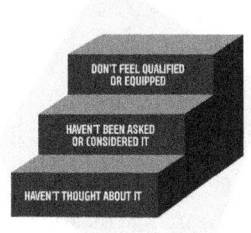

Solving the Problem

When someone who isn't new in their faith is not making disciples, who is responsible? Put more bluntly, when disciples aren't making disciples who is to blame?

The knee-jerk answer is: they are. If someone is a disciple of Jesus and they aren't being obedient to the Great Commission then it's on them. For the past hundred years the first approach to getting a non-disciple maker to start making disciples has been to take them to Matthew 28:18-20 and

The Bicycle Illustration

show them that Jesus *commanded* it. And if He *commanded* it, then a disciple can have only one response—to do it.

But perhaps the knee-jerk answer isn't the best answer. Perhaps it's those who *are* making disciples who are to blame for those who are not. After all, if 83% of those who aren't making disciples are saying that they either haven't thought about it, been asked to do it, or been equipped to do it, then disciple makers surely bear some responsibility.

If you aren't making disciples because you don't feel qualified or equipped or perhaps no one has suggested it to you then this booklet is for you.

I've been making disciples for decades now and I've learned some principles and practices that will help equip you. My hope is that by the end you will no longer say, or believe, that you aren't qualified or equipped or that no one has suggested it to you.

In this booklet I will introduce you to an illustration that has become a game changer for many disciples. The illustration is simple yet powerful. It enfolds many disciple making principles into an image that's familiar and transferable. As you grasp the illustration and its implications, you'll be well on your way to being a fruitful disciple maker. One aspect of the illustration that's been most helpful is how it answers many of the first questions young and would-be disciple makers ask.

In this booklet you can expect answers to six questions:

1. What is a disciple?
2. How do I know if I'm ready to make a disciple?
3. Who should I invite into a disciple making relationship?
4. How do I invite someone into a disciple making relationship (in a way that isn't weird)?
5. What should I do when I disciple someone?
6. How do I know when that person is ready to disciple someone else?

Becoming a disciple maker can start with this simple truth: *Making a ᐧisciple is just like riᐧing a bike.*

The Bicycle Illustration

The Bicycle Illustration

As you may know, bicycle literally means, "two wheels." The wheels of a bicycle are what make it a bicycle. Two wheels support everything else and connect the rest of the bicycle to the road. Like a bicycle, disciple making starts with the wheels.

The Back Wheel: The Disciple's Wheel

The back wheel is the wheel of power and stability on a bicycle. As the chain hooks around the sprocket it allows the bike to be powered. Since the back wheel is locked in place and doesn't move from side to side, it can move only forward or backward.

The back wheel is the stable part of disciple making as well. Our relationship with God must be the stable and unwavering part of making disciples. It is our life with Jesus that we have to offer those we disciple. If there's no stable, dynamic connection to Him then we have nothing to which we can anchor our disciple making.

The Bicycle Illustration

THE DISCIPLE'S WHEEL

Adapted from The Wheel ©1969 by The Navigators. Used by permission of The Navigators. All rights reserved.

The Navigators' Wheel[2] is useful in explaining what the life of a disciple should look like. For that reason, I sometimes call the Wheel Illustration the "disciple's wheel." It provides a useful image of the life of a disciple. The center, or hub, is Jesus.

In the life of a disciple, Jesus is central. He is the one whose sinless life, death on the cross, and resurrection from the dead allows each person to have a relationship with God. By faith, we are able to experience saving grace that brings us into a right relationship with Him. He saved us from sin and its power over us. Through Him we are able to experience eternal life that starts now and extends into eternity. He saved us not just *from* sin, but He also saved us *for* life in His Kingdom. It is our communion with Jesus that ultimately satisfies our souls in this life and the next. He is truly our greatest treasure and source of joy. Without Jesus as the center, we simply cannot be a disciple of God (1 Timothy 2:5). Just as a bicycle moves forward when the chain grabs hold of the sprocket in the center of the back wheel, so too does the disciple move forward when Jesus grabs hold of each aspect of his life bit by bit.

The spokes of a wheel connect the center to the rim. The spokes help the wheel maintain its shape and strengthen the connection between the power source and where the rubber meets the road.

A disciple of Jesus is someone who follows Jesus in order to become just like Jesus. This means she is working to become like Him in morals, methods, and movement. It's not enough for her to know what Jesus knew or to do what He did. A disciple wants to be just like Him (Luke 6:40, 1

The Bicycle Illustration 9

John 2:6). Jesus boiled the entire law of God into just two commands: love God and love others. The four spokes of the wheel focus the disciple on those two things. The vertical spokes help us love God well, while the horizontal spokes help us love others.

First let's talk about the vertical spokes.

The top spoke that comes down into the hub is that of the Word. God revealed Scripture not just to inform us, but also to form us. It's effective in teaching, rebuking, correcting, and training disciples in righteousness. Not only that, but Scripture is living and active and is designed to get into our thoughts and through our emotions so that it reaches our innermost parts. As it does so, it acts as a judge of our heart. To say it's powerful is an understatement! In fact, study after study has found that reflecting on God's word is the most effective way to help a disciple grow.

The spoke coming from the center to the bottom is prayer. Prayer is simply communication with God. While Scripture is God's written Word that has come down to us, prayer is typically seen as our communication moving up towards Him. That doesn't mean prayer is one way communication. Prayer is both talking and listening to God (John 8:47, John 10:4, Acts 22:14-15). Jesus modeled a life of prayer for His disciples. A disciple is devoted to prayer (Colossians 4:2). Most disciples find that the greatest value of prayer isn't getting God to do what they want, but helping them get to know what God wants.

The horizontal spokes help us fulfill the second part of the great commandment: to love others. These horizontal spokes divide people into those who don't yet know and follow Jesus and those who do. Since every person on the earth is in one of those categories, the horizontal spokes help us remember to love both the skeptics and the saved.

The left spoke is witnessing, or sharing our faith with those who don't follow Jesus. After all, Jesus came to seek and to save those who were harassed, lost, and struggling in life (Matthew 9:36-38, Luke 19:10). He was often criticized for being too close to and spending too much time with those who were far from God and not the "religious types." He loved them so much He not only spent time with them, He loved that time! And they loved His presence. Since disciples are those who are trying to be just like Jesus, it's important for each

The Bicycle Illustration

disciple to intentionally build relationships with non-Christians. We can't be like Him if we don't and we can't make disciples if we never reach those who have yet to find life in Him.

The right spoke is all about loving other Christians. Each disciple is part of God's family, the Church, which Paul calls the Body (1 Corinthians 12, Romans 12). Every disciple is called to engage the world (witnessing), and also to care for other believers (Galatians 6:1-10). Typically this looks like relational involvement in a network of believers (a church), while using one's gifts to build up and equip others in that local body. Service, hospitality, and helping others grow in their faith are a few ways that disciples can love other Christians. Two common words that describe loving other Christians are community and fellowship.

One more thing about spokes: because they are designed to support the shape of the wheel, they need to stay in balance with one another. If one spoke becomes much bigger than the others then the wheel will become warped and won't roll smoothly. In the same way, each of these four spokes should be fairly proportional in a disciple's life.

Finally, the outside of the wheel, or the rim, is where "the rubber meets the road." In the life of a disciple the rim is where understanding meets action. It's the place of obedience. Too often Christians get stuck learning about the spokes and never get to the rim. Such a wheel isn't really a wheel at all because it stays on the level of concepts and understanding instead of action. That kind of wheel won't get you anywhere! James warns us against this danger when he says, "Do not merely listen to the word…do what it says!" (James 1:22). Too often Christians believe this:

More information = More transformation

In reality, transformation depends on application:

Information + Application = Transformation.

Just as the back bicycle wheel is meant for motion, so is a disciple. As he lives his life others may not see him practice each spoke, but they should be able to see the difference that Jesus (the hub) makes in his life and the way Jesus impacts his choices (the rim). As with a wheel in motion, we no longer see the spokes but rather the hub and rim that they attach to.

So the back wheel is the disciple's wheel, the wheel of stability. It's the wheel that powers our relationship with God and others—and certainly the disciple making relationship. The back wheel helps us understand that a disciple is someone whose life is centered on Jesus and the priorities he modeled and taught.

The Front Wheel: The Disciple Maker's Wheel

The front wheel is known as the disciple maker's wheel (also known as the disciple maker's loop). Like the back wheel it moves forward and backwards, but it can also turn side to side, which sets the direction for the whole bike. For that reason, I call it the wheel of steering and vision. The disciple maker's wheel clarifies the process of disciple making into six steps. In other words, it answers the question, "What do I do when I disciple someone?"

Since the goal of a disciple and a disciple maker is to become just like Jesus, the center of the front wheel, like the back, is Jesus. In fact, centering both wheels on Jesus as the hub reminds us that the perfect way to make a disciple is Jesus' way. So the goal as a disciple maker is to do what He did. But what exactly did Jesus do to help His disciples move from ordinary fishermen to those who had walk-on-water faith?

THE DISCIPLE MAKER'S WHEEL

The disciple maker's wheel has six spokes:

The Bicycle Illustration

teach him what, tell her why, show him how, get her started, keep him going, and help her pass it on. These simple steps are useful for every aspect of disciple making. They help bring practical focus to the process of disciple making. To further illustrate and explain these steps, let's look at each step as it pertains to the topic of prayer.

1. Teach Him What: The first step of the loop is to teach what the topic is about. So, what is prayer? This teaching helps the disciple understand prayer. Teaching is the most common aspect of discipleship. It's the reason most disciples' knowledge outpaces their practice. Still, teaching is important (2 Timothy 3:16) and should be done well.

2. Tell Her Why: After she understands what prayer is she needs to know why it's important. Answering "why" helps a disciple build inner conviction and motivation. A skilled discipler addresses the why through both the Scriptures (Acts 17:11) and through experience and personal testimony. Prayer is important not just because Scripture says it is but also because of the difference it makes in my life. Personal testimony puts flesh on doctrine and encourages the disciple to follow suit.

3. Show Him How: It's not enough to teach him what prayer is and why it's important, he also needs to experience it with you. If you want him to pray, then you must show him how to pray. Practically that looks like praying together and explaining what you're doing and why. Whether you use the ACTS acronym (Adoration, Confession, Thanksgiving, Supplication), the Lord's prayer (Matthew 6:9-13), or another method, doing it together makes a huge difference because in disciple making more is caught by observation and experience than is intentionally taught.

4. Get Her Started: Now that you've taught what, told why, and shown how, she needs to start her own practice. This goal-setting step should be done cooperatively. Asking simple questions such as, "How many days this week do you think you could have an intentional prayer time?" and "About how long do you want to make each session?" help the disciple set attainable goals. In addition to asking questions, during this step, the discipler should focus on encouraging at this point. Seeking to join her for one of these prayer times also shows your care for her and priority of application here.

5. Keep Him Going: Since the goal is trans-

The Bicycle Illustration

formation, just a week or two of prayer is not sufficient. The discipler can't stop now. He must help keep him going. A mistake many disciplers make is to assume a new practice will continue months after you focused on it. As we know from our own lives, it takes accountability and encouragement to establish new habits. Regularly revisiting topics that you've helped a person move through is an important part of the disciple maker's wheel.

6. Help Her Pass It On: Finally, the disciple needs to pass it on. Sharing with someone else what we've learned and practiced invites others into our lives and sets us up as influencers.

Additionally clear explanation is a final step towards mastery and ownership. When a disciple regularly shares new insights and skills with others she equips herself as a disciple maker. Such regular practice sets her up to make disciples without being dependent upon a discipleship curriculum.

To review then, the disciple making wheel is comprised of these six steps repeated over and over again:

1. Teach him/her what.
2. Tell him/her why.
3. Tell him/her how.

4. Get him/her started.
5. Keep him/her going.
6. Help him/her pass-it-on.

Practicing the disciple making wheel means following these six steps over and over again in different areas of the disciple's life. Repeating these steps helps the disciple maker, or discipler, know what to do in a disciple making relationship. But that's not all the disciple maker's wheel is about. Remember this is also the wheel of steering. In a disciple making relationship, steering is the responsibility of the disciple maker.

Vision

To steer effectively the disciple maker needs to understand the destination. In other words, he needs to know what he hopes the disciple will become and actively steer toward that destination. Jesus demonstrated this when he invited Peter and Andrew to follow Him, be changed by Him, and be committed to His mission (Matthew 4:19). He also demonstrated vision for the disciples when He renamed them based on their characteristics—

Peter the rock, James and John—sons of Thunder. In short, maturity aimed toward the lost is the ultimate destination (Luke 6:40, Colossians 1:28). Since the maturity of the disciple maker limits their ability to reach the destination, growth always matters. It also matters because no one can disciple beyond their own maturity. The connection between our maturity and our effectiveness makes disciple making more like sculpture than assembly. Mature disciple makers make fully formed disciples who have vision, heart, and skill in loving God and loving others well (back wheel beliefs and practices), but each one will carry that out in a way that's unique.

Another aspect of steering is responsiveness. Just as every road has turns and obstacles, the road to the final destination of mature disciples isn't straight or without hazards. The curves in the road of a disciple making relationship are the current habits, questions, and character of the disciple. Each one brings something different. One may feel a deep need to fully understand the intricacies of salvation, another may have trouble with self-discipline, another may struggle with people-pleasing, another may have sin habits that are difficult to overcome. Disciple makers must respond to the needs and wants of the disciple without turning down a side road that never leads to the destination.

Vision and responsiveness depend on focus. Just like when you steer a bike, if you only look right in front of you it's hard to maintain control or balance. Likewise, if you only look way out then you may fail to see a barrier right in front of you. A healthy focus in a disciple making relationship is a balance of both.

The Frame

Now that we've covered the two wheels, it's time to focus on the frame. The frame connects the wheels to one another and provides structure and support to the rider. Taken together it allows everything to work well together.

In disciple making the frame does the same thing. It provides structure, support, and connection. On most bicycles the frame is made up of two triangles. For the purposes of this illustration, the smaller triangle closest to the back wheel tells us who we should invite into a disciple making relationship. The larger triangle that's closer to the front wheel tells us what disciple making involves and helps us understand how to invite someone into a disciple making relationship. Let's start by looking at the smaller triangle close to the back wheel.

The Small Triangle: Who to Invite?

Inviting someone into a disciple making relationship can be intimidating. Some fear rejection, others fear being perceived as prideful, or communicating that the other person has an obvious immaturity. All too often, new disciple makers select for the wrong reasons. Some seek to minimize the risk of rejection and choose a believer they know will say yes. Others want to make sure they'll be needed, so they choose a spiritual orphan who has big needs in his life. And still others, seek to guarantee they'll know enough to help so they choose a much younger or less wise person. In each case the reasoning is understandable, but worldly wisdom often leads to spiritual frustration.

Disciple makers need to be led by God in the selection process. Prayer is a big part of that. Jesus prayed all night before selecting the Twelve (Luke 6:12-16). The disciples prayed before deciding Matthias would replace Judas (Acts 1:24-26). Selection is important and those who aren't careful will learn the hard way that it's easier to invite someone to come along than it is to ask them to go away. So, what should a disciple maker consider before selecting someone to disciple?

Disciple Makers all over the world have learned

The Bicycle Illustration

an acronym that forms the minimum basic requirements for a disciple to be a good candidate for a disciple making relationship. That acronym is F – A – T.

F stands for faithfulness. It's a way to measure trustworthiness to both God and to current growth opportunities.

Luke 16:10 helps us understand the importance of faithfulness. It says, *"He who is faithful in a very little thing is also faithful in much; and he who is unrighteous in a very little thing is unrighteous also in much."*[3] Faithfulness is an indicator of whether a person can be trusted to steward something. Do you want to know how a person will respond to the opportunity of being discipled? Observe how that person currently handles growth opportunities (corporate worship/teaching, small groups, training opportunities, etc.). This is the best indicator of how he'll handle the new opportunity of being discipled. Those who are faithful with what they already have may be ready for more.

A stands for availability. It's a way to measure a person's priorities.

As you talk with those you're considering,

which ones are loudly (& perhaps proudly) proclaiming their busyness? A person who can barely find time to meet with you for their own growth, is unlikely to find time to disciple someone else. Since we all make time for what's most important to us, busyness is actually a priority issue.

T stands for teachability. This is a way to measure both humility and hunger.

Let's face it, some people are more interested in conversation and connection than in transformation. They seem content with where they are in their faith. Others may have the hunger to grow, but distrust everyone who isn't their favorite Christian celebrity. As you spend time around a potential person to disciple do they seem hungry to learn? Are they eager to learn *from you*? It's important not to confuse teachability with a willingness to jettison their beliefs for yours. The Bereans were praised by Paul because they didn't simply trust what he taught, but instead they checked it against Scripture. Teachability is a genuine desire to learn and grow, but it's also a commitment to wrestle with different viewpoints in order to become like Him.

The Large Triangle: How to Invite

When I invite someone into a discipling relationship, I begin by sharing how being discipled changed my life. Through story, I share about the impact Greg made on me twenty years ago. If you've never been discipled then just begin by explaining what God's been doing in you to get you to this point. Next, I explain what I'm inviting them to do with me. In short, I say that a disciple making relationship involves three things.

The first side is relationship building. Disciple making starts with a relationship. It's not a class, Bible study, or book club. I explain to the person that disciple making is meant to be two (or more) people learning and caring for one another while they try to follow Jesus. To that end, part of disciple making is becoming actual friends who relate with trust and openness.

The second side of the triangle is life and ministry skills. Much of what is talked about in the disciple making relationship fits into one of these categories. A life skill is something that anyone in our culture needs to develop, whether they follow Jesus or not. Examples include money management, conflict resolution, parenting skills, etc. Ministry skills are needs that are specific to Christ followers. Examples include how to understand Scripture, how to share about Jesus, how to disciple others, etc.

Finally the third side of this triangle is character development. Over time, as we build a

The Bicycle Illustration 27

relationship of trust, we will notice things about the other person that are not in alignment with who Jesus is or what He taught. Often these things are subtle and hidden from us but obvious to those around us. Examples include needing to be the center of attention, always taking the best seat at small group, insecurity that leads to social isolation, etc. As we disciple, we commit to bringing them up to the other person as lovingly and as gently as we can.

After explaining that each of these three really make up a disciple making relationship. I ask, "Which of these three do you think is most often left out and why?"

After decades of asking that question, people normally say #1 or #3. I believe it's #3 – character development – because it's not fun for anyone. I can still remember the mixture of anger and shock I felt when my discipler asked why I hadn't gotten up to help clear the table the week before. Almost everyone else at the meeting had, but I sat and talked with a friend. It hurt and I was defensive, but I tried to listen. At the end of our conversation, he gently asked me if I would ask God about that incident and whether or not I needed to respond to what he had observed. I did ask God, and He made it clear that I needed to grow so that I served like Jesus did. Truth is, I'm still working to develop in that area.

Being on the other side of character development is no fun either. Pointing out a character flaw to someone you deeply care about is a labor of love. As difficult as it is, these conversations have incredible transformational power. Even though it's hard, it's a tangible example of loving someone enough to tell them something that others see, but are unwilling to confront.

I move this invitational conversation to a close by affirming the person and how I've seen God at work in his life. In short, I explain why I think he'd be a good fit for disciple making. Next, I ask if he has any questions. If not, I ask him to pray about it and set up a time for a follow-up conversation in the near future.

In the next conversation, if he's interested, commit to meeting together for only a couple months. This "try-it-on" period protects you from committing to someone who isn't FAT. It also allows him the opportunity to see if the relationship will be what you've described. At the end of that period, assess how things are going. Regardless of how it's going after those two months, it's important to have that conversation. If both of you think it's going well, then it's affirming and builds momentum. If one or both of you think it's not going well, then you have the opportunity to course correct or simply stop meeting.

The three sides of this triangle—relationship building, life and ministry skills, and character development—helps open a conversation that can be scary or awkward. I've found that this approach is affirming and honoring to everyone, even to those who decide not to do it.

Balance: Relationship & Intentionality

Now that we've covered both wheels and the frame, we need to talk about balance. In learning to ride a bike, not falling off to one side or another is one of the hardest skills to master. In fact, if you can't keep your balance then you can't really ride a bike. It is that important. It also protects the rider from being hurt, because losing your balance and falling is dangerous and hurts!

In disciple making balance is just as important. Instead of falling to the right or left, as is the case in bike riding, in disciple making you can fall to one side by being too intentional or to the other side by being too relational. Both relationship and intentionality are needed, but too much or too little of either derails the whole disciple making process. All falls aren't equal though, falling toward the road is more dangerous than falling away from it. In the same way, losing balance because you have too much intentionality is more dangerous than too much relationship.

Too much intentionality in a disciple making relationship will cause the interaction to feel overly formal and knowledge driven. When this happens the person being discipled often feels like a project, rather than a person. Too much intentionality creates a cold environment for disciple making and while some will endure it to soak up the information and continue in the relationship, many will simply quit or disappear. When this happens, the disciple maker can feel confused and frustrated. Worse yet, they may conclude that the disciple had a problem being faithful, which gives the disciple maker license

The Bicycle Illustration

to disciple the next person without reflection or changing their methods.

Falling away from the road by having too much relationship in disciple making is also dangerous. At first glance, it seems counter-intuitive that there could be too much relationship. After all, isn't loving one another a major part of being and making disciples? Of course, it is, but disciple making is more than friendship. Jesus didn't invite the disciples to simply be with Him, but also to be sent out on mission (Mark 3:14, Matthew 4:19, et al). When disciple making takes the form of friendship then it's dangerous to both the disciple and the disciple maker. Unlike falling to the side of intentionality, people will generally stay in the disciple making relationship, but are branded with a picture of disciple making that's different from what Jesus modeled. The result is disciple making that lacks the power of Jesus-style disciple making!

So falling to either side of too much intentionality or too much relationship stops the progress of multiplying disciple makers who look and multiply like Jesus.

Brake: Pace and Reflection

Bicycles have brakes to stop or slow down. Braking is necessary because the slope of life or your pedaling can make you go faster than you can safely maintain. Alternatively, obstacles sometimes appear that require you to slow down so that you can safely maneuver around them without crashing.

In disciple making brakes are important as well. At times, the pace of disciple making needs to change because an obstacle has come up in the life of the disciple. Health problems, marital struggles, the birth of a child, or losing a job are all examples of obstacles that require slowing down to safely navigate through.

Disciple makers should also periodically hit the brakes to assess how the disciple making relationship is going. Taking the time to ask questions about how the relationship is going from both sides allows for insight to emerge and adjustments to be made. Disciple making without braking for reflection and can lead to disaster or simply cause you to miss the destination.

Seat & Handle Bars: The Posture of a Disciple Maker

The next parts of a bicycle are the seat and handle bars. These are easy to overlook because their utility is so obvious. When it comes to riding a bike the height and distance of these two parts are directly connected to the rider's posture.

The posture a person has when riding a bicycle impacts their ability to stay in-balance and to ride for long distances. When it comes to disciple making our posture in the relationship is important and directly impacts our balance. Are we making disciples for our own ego or for God's glory? Do we understand God's role and our role in the disciple making relationship? Are we trusting our own ability, skill, and experience or are we trusting in the Holy Spirit to lead, guide, and provide the growth?

Another way to say this is, are you discipling others WITH God or just FOR God? Healthy disciple making is acknowledging the co-creative process occurring between three persons, the disciple, the disciple maker, and the Holy Spirit. It's possible to master every other part of the bicycle and still not reach the destination because of fatigue or loss of interest. By holding onto the handlebars loosely and sitting expectantly (of what God will do) a disciple maker can engage the disciple appropriately for the whole journey.

In disciple making, fruitfulness flows out of our intimate connection with Jesus (John 15:4).

This way of entering and holding a disciple making relationship stands in contrast to simply moving a disciple through a book or curriculum. If the steering is left to chapters of extra-Biblical content then the disciple maker is relegated to the role of a book-jockey. Disciple making requires discernment and attention that is the result of being a disciple, not just knowing things.

Destination and Vision

Bicycles are made to take us from here to there. Whether you ride a bike as a mode of transportation or enjoyment, going somewhere is the point. In disciple making the destination that is spelled out for us is expressed in several places in Scripture. Habakkuk 2:14 says, *"...for the earth will be fille, with the knowle,ge of the glory of the Lor, as the waters cover the sea."* A similar thought is expressed in Romans 14:11 which says that, *"every knee shall bow to me, an, every tongue shall confess to Go,."*

Just like looking at the ground right in front of a cyclist will lead to a wreck, the discipler needs to keep their eyes set on the final destination. At the end, every person will bow their knee with the knowledge that Jesus is Lord over all. Disciple making is the way God has directed us to help others. It's a way that we worship Him, but also a way that we bring others into that worship. Disciple making is much more than a responsibility, it's a great privilege.

Just Like Riding a Bike

The bicycle illustration is effective in helping new and young disciple makers get started in disciple making. And I'm confident that if you apply them they will help you too.

As we saw previously, the Barna study concludes that the biggest obstacle to non-disciple makers becoming disciple makers is individuals not feeling qualified or equipped. In response I've seen pastors and para-church ministries allocate tremendous time and energy toward developing and launching resources to help fill that equipping gap. Not only are resources being created, but much thought is being given to how to get these resources in the hands of those who need them most.

These resources are well-crafted and insightful. They are being consumed and appreciated by thousands, but they aren't making disciple makers. Unfortunately, the obstacle that non-disciple

The Bicycle Illustration

makers feel is not the obstacle that's keeps them from making disciples.

Don't get me wrong, I fully believe non-disciple makers feel unprepared and unequipped, but it's just not what keeps them from making disciples.

Justin G. Gravitt

Beyond the Illustration

Unfortunately the biggest obstacle faced by non-disciple makers isn't going to be solved by resources or even the bicycle illustration. No matter how clearly these helpful principles are expressed individuals can still honestly say, I don't feel qualified or equipped.

It makes perfect sense because disciple making is like riding a bike.

No matter how much training you get or how many books you read or how many workshops you attend people can still honestly say that they don't know how. The reason is simple, learning to ride a bike or learning to make a disciple only happens by doing it.

Disciple making requires more than just an interest in learning about it. It requires the courage to actually put that learning into action.

It's actually, just. Like. Riding. a Bike.

Do you remember learning to ride a bike? Perhaps you helped someone else learn to ride a bike? If so you know that it's a unique experience. Do you remember that strange mix of wanting to learn and not wanting to learn? The combination of intense interest and palpable fear?

I have taught each of my four kids how to ride a bike and for each one it was a bit different, but each one had to overcome a common obstacle: fear. And this fear wasn't your average everyday fear, it was what I call two-faced fear. Two-faced fear is the simultaneous fear of failing and the fear of succeeding. And in disciple making and bike riding it's the main obstacle that must be overcome.

When you're learning to ride a bike, failure hurts—a lot. Falling results in scraped knees, elbows, and sometimes even bumps on your forehead. Fear of pain is a strong deterrent to riding a bike. And it keeps some from ever learning it. When asked, why they don't ride a bike, they can honestly say that they don't know how! But even though it's true, the real reason is fear has kept them from trying.

Fear of failure keeps many from trying to make disciples too. The dynamics are similar. The person imagines the pain of failure and wants to avoid it. In disciple making many envision others not wanting to learn from them or being asked a question they don't know the answer to or simply being in an uncomfortable situation they

The Bicycle Illustration

don't know how to handle. When asked why they don't make disciples they too honestly say they don't know how!

The other side of fear that comes in disciple making and bike riding is the fear of success. In the beginning stages of riding a bike most have a parent, sibling, or friend nearby to steady them if they start to fall. But as skill increases so does the danger—at least in the short term. As the bike goes faster the helper is left behind and now a fall is *really* going to hurt. Many get to this stage and discover a problem they'd never considered before, "how am I going to stop this thing?!"

In disciple making the fear of success is similar. What if it all goes fine, but I'm doing it "wrong?" What if I teach something wrong? What if I'm good at it and then people are multiplying things that are a bit off? What if I'm not good at it, and the disciples never disciple anyone else?

In many instances, the fear of success is really the fear of partial success. It's the fear of making progress only to realize there are other challenges and problems that had never been considered. In many ways, it's the fear of the unknown that lurk around every corner.

Two-faced fear stares down every would-be disciple maker and must be overcome.

The Dad Guarantee

At the beginning of this booklet I asked this: When disciples aren't making disciples who is to blame? Put another way, when someone who isn't new in the faith isn't making disciples then who is responsible?

I proposed then that, disciple makers bear the responsibility. After all, if we know how to do it, then we have to be the ones to explain and to train those who do not. I still believe that's true, but it's not the whole picture.

Eventually, the responsibility for not making disciples shifts to those not making disciples. The irony of a booklet like this is that explanation can never take the place of application. In order to become a disciple maker then you need to start discipling someone. If you want to start discipling someone then you need to overcome the two-faced fear that you feel and start doing it.

So how do you overcome two-faced fear? For my kids the key was the Dad Guarantee.

The Bicycle Illustration

When I took my kids to learn to ride their bike I'd start by asking them the same question, "How are you feeling?" "Scared," they'd say. We'd talk about their fear. Then we'd talk about how great it would be to be able to ride a bike and how fun it would be. Finally, I'd look them in the eye and say, "Listen you don't need to be afraid right now because you can't fall." At this point I'd have them climb into the seat and say, "Go ahead and lean, try to fall." They'd lean with all their might to one side or the other and I'd hold the back of the seat and the handle bars and keep them from falling. "See," I'd say, "You can't fall, it's a Dad guarantee and a Dad guarantee never fails."

The Dad Guarantee never failed to bring a smile to their face and it never disappointed.
It helped them learn the basics of balance and posture, steering and vision, without the fear of falling.

Eventually though, they were ready for me to start letting go. So I told them, "Ok, you're really getting the hang of this. So, you're ready for the next part of the Dad guarantee. You're ready for me to start letting go. I can no longer promise that you won't fall, but I promise if you do, I'll be right here with you."

This part of the conversation never brought a smile, but we'd talk through it. I'd tell them they were ready and I knew they could do it. And off they went. Next came the falls, the scraped knees, and the bruises. And every time I was right there to pick them up and dust them off.

God's Dad Guarantee

Will you start making disciples? I'm not the only one asking, Jesus is asking you to do it, too.

His ask is found in His final words. In Matthew 28, the eleven disciples met the resurrected Jesus on a mountain in Galilee. They saw Him, worshipped Him, and some still doubted.

Hey, maybe we would have, too! They'd been through so much. It's amazing to think about what the disciples were feeling in those moments. He was with them again. Back from the grave. Imagine the anticipation they would have felt as He started to talk to them. They couldn't know what He'd say, but they were definitely hanging on every word.

"All authority in heaven and earth has been given to me. Therefore, go and make disciples of all nations, baptizing them in the name of the Father, and of the Son, and of the Holy Spirit, and teaching them to obey everything I have commanded you. And surely I'm with you to the very end of the age."

Did you know that when Jesus asked His disciples to make disciples that He was asking you, too? It's true because when Jesus asked the disciples to make disciples He told them to do it by teaching the new disciples *to obey everything* that Jesus taught. And part of everything is making disciples. So that mandate has traveled down through the millennia to you. And to me.

Isn't that exciting? Isn't that…scary? If you've never made a disciple, the very thought of doing it causes two-faced fear to raise its ugly head. The good news is I think God has given us His "Dad guarantee" to help us overcome two-faced fear.

The first part is found at the beginning of the Great Commission. Jesus says, "All authority in heaven and earth has been given to me. Therefore, go…" we can take that in a couple different ways. We could take it harshly, as in, "Hey I want you to know that I have ALL authority so, you better get to it or else!" or we could take it as a promise of success, "Hey, I want you to know that I have ALL authority. It doesn't matter what your boss thinks or what the government says or even what obstacles are in your way. I hold *all authority*, so go ahead, I've got your back." Which one do you think is more consistent with God and His character?

Jesus has your back in disciple making. It's the

The Bicycle Illustration   47

first part of His "Dad Guarantee" for us. As you take your first scary steps towards making disciples you can know that you are working with and in His authority. In that authority He will strengthen and sustain you (Isaiah 41:10). Authority to make disciples is especially important because Satan will often try to convince you that you aren't ready, you don't know enough, and that your life is too messed up to help others.

His authority doesn't mean that you won't fail or encounter difficult and painful situations as you disciple. But that's where the second part of God's "Dad Guarantee" comes in. He says, "And surely, I will be with you always, to the very end of the age." This part of the guarantee is essentially the same promise I give to my kids when teaching them to ride a bike. Jesus promises to be right there as you go. He knows that as you go there will be times that you feel like you're in over your head. There will be times when you fall and end up with scrapes and bruises, but no matter what, He'll be right there with you.

When you combine the two parts of God's "Dad guarantee" with the Holy Spirit that empowers us, you have what you need to overcome the two-faced fear that seeks to keep us from making disciples.

Ready to Ride?

Today all four of my kids are bike riders. Each one had to overcome two-faced fear. They've had to face it in other areas of their life, too, like when they learned to swim, went to a sports try-out, and so on. Chances are you've overcome two-faced fear in some areas of your life too. In order to become a disciple maker, you'll need to do it again. Your feelings of insecurity, lack of equipping, or preparation are not reliable measures of your actual readiness to disciple others.

I know because not long ago, an ice-breaker led to a break-through. It happened, when I was in a room of 150 highly experienced and highly capable disciple makers. At our tables of ten we were asked to share how we got started as disciple makers. As I listened to each person share a common theme emerged. Every one of us started making disciples in spite of feeling scared and not ready. Not one of us felt qualified or equipped. We were unsure about our ability, our readiness, and yes, even our

The Bicycle Illustration 49

equipping. Come to think of it, that's how I felt when I got on a bicycle for the first time.

Let me assure you, if you are walking with God then you are ready to make a disciple. You don't have to have it all figured out. Your life doesn't have to be figured out or all cleaned up. You just need to be one step ahead of the person you will disciple. To get started you don't need to know more. You don't need to read another book. You don't need to go to a disciple making workshop. And you don't need to be discipled first.

But don't take my word for it. God wants to make sure you know it. He's given you His "Dad Guarantee" saying, "All authority in heaven and on earth has been given to me. Therefore go and make disciples of all nations, baptizing them in the name of the Father and of the Son and of the Holy Spirit, and teaching them to obey everything I have commanded you. And surely I am with you always, to the very end of the age."

And if you're still not convinced of your readiness consider, 2 Peter 1:3, *"His divine power has given us everything we need for a godly life through our knowledge of him who called us by his own glory and goodness."* You have *everything* you need to do what God has called you to do.

Learning to make disciples is like learning to ride a bike. It starts with confidence in your Father, not yourself. As you look to God, you'll learn that He is faithful to help you overcome two-faced fear. And as you do you'll go places and do things you never imagined!

1. ^ https://www.barna.com/research/christians-discipleship-community/ accessed 5/5/2023
2. Wheel Illustration used with permission, copyright The Navigators 1969. All rights reserved. The original Wheel Illustration (shown below) was developed by The Navigators' founder, Dawson Trotman in the 1930's.

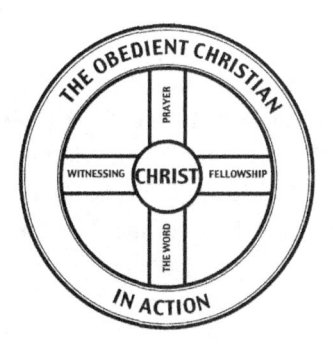

3. All Scripture quotations, unless otherwise indicated, are taken from the Holy Bible, New International Version,® NIV.® Copyright © 1973, 1978, 1984, 2011 by Biblica, Inc.® All rights reserved worldwide.

ABOUT THE AUTHOR

Justin Gravitt is a disciple making leader and writer whose primary passion is to help everyday believers repurpose their lives in light of God's plan for them as disciple-makers. Justin has served with The Navigators since 2000, and is the founder and executive director of the Dayton Disciple Makers Network, host of the popular Practitioners' Podcast, and author of The Foundation of a Disciplemaking Culture (NavPress 2024). He's an avid Reds fan, loves the beach, and Dad-joking his kids. He lives in Dayton, Ohio, with his wife, Kristen, and their four children.

To connect with him or to learn more, visit his website at www.justingravitt.com

Designed by: *Lauren Pyles*

PylesDesign.net